WHAT'S YOUR MOTIVATION

Values Matter

Annette R. Johnson

allwrite
advertising & publishing

Published by:
 Allwrite Advertising and Publishing
P.O. Box 1071
Atlanta, Georgia 30301 USA
www.allwritepublishing.com

You can find more exercises at www.whatmotivation.com Click the "Surveys" tab.

ISBN: 978-0-9844931-6-6

CONTENTS

INTRODUCTION

Survival is a matter of how you respond to change.
-Charles Darwin

This workbook was created as a supplement to the book *"What's Your Motivation?: Identifying and Understanding What Drives You."* It tackles values and how they affect our choices, especially when it comes to change. While change is an inevitable part of life, some treat it as optional, resisting and pretending until its existence brings undeniable consequences.

Each chapter of the workbook is designed to challenge your current sensibilities and move you toward a transition that has been delayed, diverted or denied. Chapter 1 begins with an overview of change and its general obstacles. The workbook goes on to identify what we have come to believe will cause change in our lives – information.

The L.I.E. Process provides the central means to change, which, as diagrammed, should be continual. From that point, you will be introduced to the three elements of change and examine their impact individually on your life. What you'll discover is that one of these three elements is the reason for your resistance or stagnation. The third element, motivation, moves us to Chapter 4's in-depth discussion and exercises on determining your core values. In this chapter, you'll also better understand the Value Matrix, which was originally introduced in the main book. This chapter is especially useful because, not only can you discover your main values, you can discover what specific value(s) can ultimately motivate you to consistent action toward any goal.

Chapter 5 solely focuses on how to overcome your distractions by using personalized fasts and conditioning new habits. The next chapter helps you to become both efficient and effective using limited and limitless resources. Finally, Chapter 7 outlines a new DIAT for a more successful life in which desire, focus and motivation are readily employed to achieve any goal.

This workbook and the exercises within it are meant to become constant reminders of your potential. Thus, you will not only be able to clearly answer what motivates you, but you will also be able to change your motivation to align with your most important undertaking – your purpose.

For religious or church groups, Chapter 8 was incorporated so that believers' values can be assessed in line with God's will, ways and worship. This chapter features facilitator-guided exercises and also offers tips to leaders who will guide a group.

1. <u>CHANGE</u>

We are usually motivated to change for only two reasons:

- Opportunity to gain something we value
- Possibility of losing something we value

General Obstacles

Even with a strong desire to change, we have personal obstacles that may interfere with the process. This includes:

- Pride   "I'm right, though."

- Fear   "Suppose I fail."

- Faith   "I don't have any money, time…"

- Sloth   "I don't feel like it now."

- Ignorance   "I don't know how."

- Attitude   "I can't do it."

The Truth About Change

We have no control over other people unless they give it to us.

God doesn't do for us what we can do for ourselves. He handles the impossible.

Change without a goal in mind leaves you at the mercy of whims.

The change many people seek involves finding their purpose. Working toward our purpose involves our whole being:

Body – do (instincts)

Mind – think (logic, conscious)

Heart – feel (emotions, subconscious)

Spirit – energy (supernatural power)

Soul – meaning (purpose)

Like people, business must sometimes change. It's called "rebanding."

What's something in your control that you've tried to do, but it seems impossible to change?

---

2. INFORMATION DIET

"Information" is what we have commonly come to believe causes change. It is provided to us in many forms, including:

- Lessons taught in schools, churches and at home
- Hypotheses provided by analysts, specialists and researchers
- Advice shared or truths explained by experts
- Discoveries announced by scientists and inventors
- Observations witnessed via the media and real life
- Secrets told by friends, revealed by family and uncovered in the media
- Testimonials given by overcomers and victims

1. What sources of information do you rely on most?

_____

2. How has it helped you?

_____

We live in the Information Age where we can access data, details, examples or answers to just about anything. Despite all this readily available help, people today suffer more from preventable occurrences than any other time in history. Here are examples of just such instances:

- **Divorce** – the U.S. has the world's highest divorce rate
- **Never married** – the rise of the never-married group ages 20-44 grew from 5% in 1970 to just 20% in 2010
- **Obesity** – the U.S. is the highest-ranking industrialized country for obesity, ranking at number 9
- **Poverty** – the number of Americans living paycheck to paycheck is up to 77%
- **Suicide** – the suicide rate is higher than the homicide rate and is the ninth leading cause of death in the U.S.
- **Cancer** – more women die from smoking-induced lung cancer in the U.S. than from breast cancer
- **Crime** – is the U.S. has the highest incarceration rate in the world

Has information alone changed us for the better? No, it hasn't! The problem is that when we get new information, we have the "challenge to change." The following seven reasons are specific obstacles to change:

- Forgetfulness or Distractions
- Fear or Lack of Faith
- False Beliefs or Negative Outlook
- False Promises or Lack of Integrity
- Feigning Comprehension or Lack of Understanding
- Facet of Culture/Lifestyle and Congregation (Family and Friends)
- Fanatical Behavior or Lack of Self-Control

Challenge to Change =

"How to Convert Information into Sustained Action to Achieve a Goal"

Consider the obstacles to change discussed previously, what are your main obstacles?

_____

_____

_____

_____

The L.I.E. Process to Change

Change is a process that should include:

1. **Learn** – get the information you need to implement change efficiently
2. **Implement** – act on what you've learned
3. **Examine** – analyze the results to determine if it worked or is working effectively

This is a continuous process that never really ends because learning should never end. The problem with learning is that it is most often informative rather transformative. Implementation of information, or change, should be a byproduct of learning. Examining changes you have made is another form of learning that should lead to more efficient implementation.

Here is the L.I.E. Model for change below:

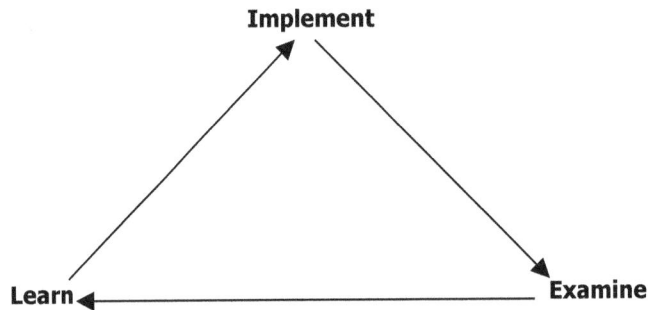

Implement

Learn   **Examine**

What step in the process do you have the most challenges in achieving? Why?

_____

_____

_____

_____

_____

_____

3. ELEMENTS OF CHANGE

Three elements are required for change:

1. **Desire** (Value)

2. **Focus** (Goal)

3. **Energy** (Motivation)

If you have failed to change, the problem is in one, two or all three areas. Each of these areas is interdependent. Having a strong desire, for instance, will be enough to cause focus and generate sufficient energy. Similarly, being deficient in one facet can interfere with the others. Here are some scenarios:

People with <u>desire and energy</u> but who lack focus are/have

- involved in a lot of activities
- easily distracted
- rarely complete anything
- no well-defined priorities or responsibilities

People with <u>focus and energy</u> but who lack desire are/have

- noncommittal or apathetic
- selfish
- fearful
- low self-esteem

People with <u>desire and focus</u> but who lack energy are

- dishonest
- lazy
- procrastinators
- wasteful

Lacking Desire

People who lack desire may be hurt or fearful due to past failures. Others may be apathetic because they have a negative attitude or they simply don't understand the impact a particular change would have on their lives. If you lack desire to change, you need to find your *why* or *what value* (see Value Matrix in Chp. 4), which is typically centered around the most important things in our lives, such as: Family, Health, Job, Relationships, Safety

Solution: **Inspiration or Need**

What was something that inspired you to work toward a goal in the past?

_____

_____

Lacking Focus

People who lack focus usually have a problem saying "no" to themselves and/or others. They may have a skewed sense of responsibility or priorities, taking on too much or insignificant things. If you lack focus, you need to eliminate distractions (Chp. 5) and determine what you want to accomplish by quantifying it. Instead of merely saying "I want to lose weight," say instead, "I want to lose one pound every week for the next 12 weeks."

Solution: **Structure or Self-Discipline**

What have you done in the past to focus or remain focused on a goal?

_____

_____

Lacking Energy

People use lots of means to power their goals and dreams. Ego and arrogance are sometimes used as fuel for self-confidence, but they may cause alienation despite achievement. If you lack motivation, you should use limitless resources as your guide and limited resources as your assistant (Chp. 6).

Solution: **Coaching or Encouragement**

What have you done in the past to get or remain motivated toward a goal?

_____

_____

Your failure to change may not only be affecting you, but also the people with whom you love; for whom you are responsible; or to whom you are accountable.

A. List three things you <u>must change</u>:

     1.

     2.

     3.

If you don't change these things, what would or may be the potential effect on the following:

Family _____

Finances _____

Health _____

Relationships _____

Future _____

Personal Fulfillment _____

Other _____

_____

Why haven't you been successful in changing these things? *(Put an X in the box)*

	Desire	Focus	Energy
Must Change 1			
Must Change 2			
Must Change 3			

B. List three things you probably <u>should change</u>:

     1.

     2.

     3.

Why have you been resistant, procrastinating or haven't even attempted to change these things? *(Put an X in the box)*

	Desire	Focus	Energy
Should Change 1			
Should Change 2			
Should Change 3			

List at least one or two ways this change may be beneficial?

_____

_____

_____

_____

_____

_____

C. List at least one thing you have <u>already changed</u> in your life:

      1.

      2.

      3.

Why were you successful in changing this? *(Put an X in the box)*

	Desire	**Focus**	**Energy**
Did Change 1			
Did Change 2			
Did Change 3			

How did changing these things impact your life now and/or in the future on the following:

Family _____

Finances _____

Health _____

Relationships _____

Future _____

Personal Fulfillment _____

Other _____

_____

4. CORE VALUES

Whether we are aware of them or not, we all have **core values** (things we need or require) and **elective values** (things we want or would like). We may refer to our values as "standards."

In order to accomplish a goal, we may have to go back to our core values for inspiration. Because life can get so stressful and hectic, we sometimes bury our core values, removing them from our awareness. Some of us even confuse our elective values with our core values. When we compromise our core values, the *enemies of achievement* emerge: <u>guilt, shame, regret, fear, bitterness,</u> and <u>malice</u>.

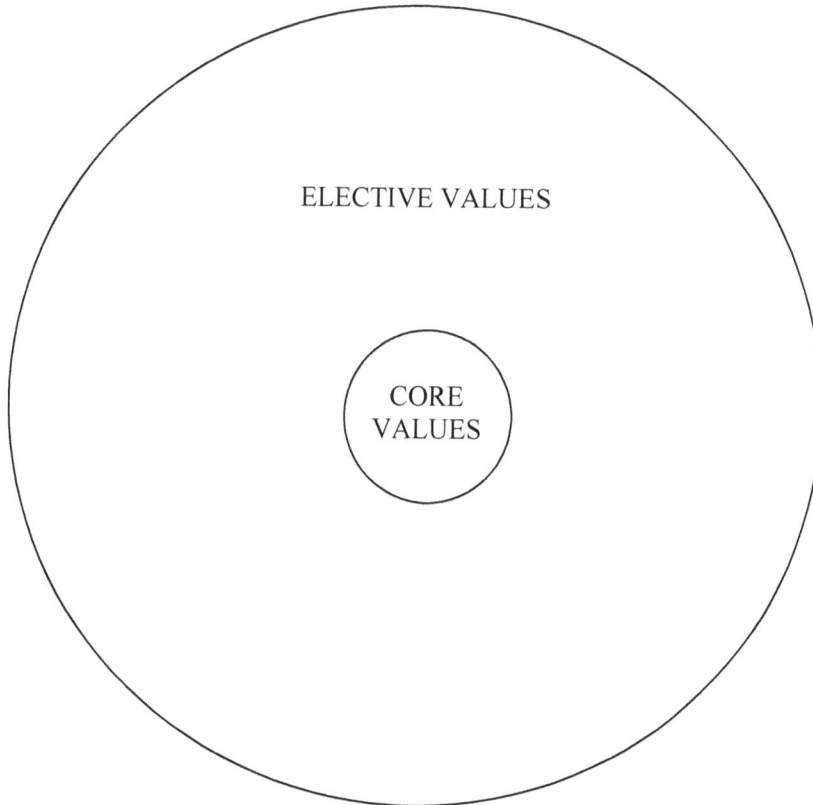

ELECTIVE VALUES

CORE
VALUES

To maximize the effectiveness of your relationships, you should know your core values and align yourself with others who share your values or have similar values.

How to Determine Core Values

1. We constantly complain about violation of our core values or standards
2. We act in an extreme manner when these values are either violated or disrespected
3. Use the Value Worksheet to determine your core values based on time, thought or money you have expended. Do it on www.whatmotivation.com

Values Matter

Motivation is whatever someone hopes to accomplish, so it compels us to act. Here is the motivational model:

$$\text{MOTIVATION} = \text{Distinct Prompt} + \text{Strong Desire} \longrightarrow \text{Response}$$

The strength of a need or desire (drive) will affect a person's preoccupation with his or her motivation. In addition, the types of prompts (cues) that can motivate people are based on their values and tastes. Thus, what motivates people is what they value most.

Here are values and cues that are associated with a person's **diet and health**:

Value	Motivation	Motivational Cue	Motivator*
Wellbeing of Person	To stay healthy; To prevent illness	*Getting sick; Food portion size; Amount of food's nutrition*	Mind
		Sports activities; Getting proper rest	Body
Appearance of Person	To look pleasing for others;	*Getting fat; Having a fit body*	Mind
	To look pleasing for oneself	*Looking good in clothes; Looking like someone else; Status; Beauty*	Heart
Taste of Food	To enjoy food	*Certain Smells; Certain Seasoning; Particular kind of food; Particular meal*	Body
Amount of Food	To have reserve or extra food; To ensure adequate amounts of food are available	*Particular meal; Seeing food; Emotional upset; Entertaining others; Togetherness; Stressful situation*	Heart
		Lacking food	Body
		Small portions	Mind
Obedience to God	To satisfy God's commands or desires; To nurture the Spirit	*Fellowship*	Spirit
		Gratitude	Heart
		Old Testament dietary rules	Mind

***Motivator** triggers feelings, thoughts, and drives. Visit www.whatmotivation.com to determine which motivator drives most of your actions or do the exercises at the back of the main book.

Here are values and cues that are associated with a person's **children**:

Value	Motivation	Motivational Cue	Motivator*
Education	To become more knowledgeable; To learn a skill; To get access to better opportunities	*Lacking understanding; Impressing others*	Mind
		Opportunity to get more information; Status	Heart
Socialization	Enjoyment; To assimilate; To be accepted	*Certain types of people; Exposure to things that seem beneficial*	Mind
		Making friends; Being part of a group; Participating in family or religious functions; Participating in sports; Peer activities	Heart
Discipline	To have good manners and self-control; To dominate or control another person	*Misbehavior; Disrespect; Poor choice*	Mind
Recreation	To enjoy competitive activities; To ensure adequate time for relaxation	*Opportunity for fun*	Heart
		Being tired	Body
		Exercise; Relieve stress	Mind
Morality	To satisfy God's commands or desires; To nurture the Spirit; To appear upstanding; To be fair	*Love for others and God*	Spirit
		Acceptance	Heart
		Rules	Mind

*Motivator triggers feelings, thoughts, and drives. Visit www.whatmotivation.com to determine which motivator drives most of your actions or do the exercises at the back of the main book.

What Do I Value Most?

Rate each value from 1 to 5 in terms of how much time, money and thought you give to it. Five (5) represents the highest. Add the totals in each row.

VALUES:	TIME	MONEY	THOUGHT	Total
Acceptance / Assimilation				
Ambition / Advancement				
Appearance				
Beauty / Art				
Competence				
Consistency				
Creativity				
Education				
Fairness				
Faith / Religion				
Family/ Children				
Food / Drink				
Freedom / Independence				
Friends				
Health				
Hobbies / Free time				
Home				
Honesty				
Humor				
Intelligence				
Job / Work				
Knowledge / Wisdom				
Love				
Money / Possessions				
New experiences / Adventure				
Personal Safety / Peace				
Pleasure / Comfort				
Power / Influence				
Prestige / Fame				
Promptness				
Recognition				
Rest / Relaxation				
Sexuality				
Social Gatherings				
Sporting Activities / Fitness				
Thrift / Saving				
Trust				
Vengeance/ Punishment				

SCORES: 1 - 3 *Low,* **4 - 6** *Somewhat,* **7 - 9** *Moderate,* **10 – 12** *Above Average,* **13 - 15** *High*

Value Matrix

The two factors that determine the motivational ability of our values are *obligation* and *awareness*. Awareness means that you consciously or purposely value something. Obligation means that you feel committed to value something.

Specific Categories

		No Obligation	Obligation
No Awareness		I. DO VALUES Accessible Convenient Natural	II. LEARNED VALUES Familial Societal Cultural
Awareness		III. SHOULD VALUES Purpose Principles Plans	IV. MUST VALUES Legal Occupational Financial

General Categories

		No Obligation	Obligation
No Awareness		I. HABITS	II. BELIEFS
Awareness		III. GOALS	IV. RESPONSIBILITIES

For our *beliefs* and *responsibilities*, which drive actions we feel obligated to do, the incentive ("what") to trigger action doesn't have to be as distinct or significant, especially for beliefs. In addition, the type of "what" depends on whether a person is internally or externally motivated.

MOTIVATION = **Distinct Incentive (What?)** + **Responsibility** ⟶ **Response**

MOTIVATION = **Indistinct Incentive (What?)** + **Belief** ⟶ **Response**

NO MOTIVATION = **No Incentive (What?)** + **Obligation** ⟶ **No Response**
(Internal/External)   (Belief/Responsibility)

For our *goals,* which represent conscious actions to which we have no obligation, the motive must be strong enough to both trigger and sustain action. This means the "why" has to be big, or effective, enough. Why has to produce enough desire to get us to focus and complete our goals.

MOTIVATION = **Goal** + **Strong Motive (Why?)** ⟶ **Response**

NO MOTIVATION = **Goal** + **Weak Motive (Why?)** ⟶ **No Response**

What is My 'What'?

What type of reward or incentive could cause you to change your behavior? If a child or an adult is behaving irresponsibly, for instance, you'll have to determine "what" he or she values most in order to trigger him/her to sustained action. If a teen values socializing, then the reward could be extra time with friends if he acts responsibly. If he fails to behave conscientiously, then the best punishment would be restriction from friends.

Once you discover the things that you value most based on the worksheet from page 18, you can create a reward system to coincide with incremental achievements toward your goal. For example:

"My goal is to keep my car clean."

I value the following:

1. Food, such as pound cake

2. Family

3. Vacationing

I can reward myself each week when I clean my car by:

1. Getting a piece of pound cake afterward

2. After one month, go on an outing with the family to our favorite place

3. After six months, take a vacation

What are some rewards you can put in place to help you get or stay motivated?

_____

_____

_____

_____

What is My 'Why'?

Go back to the three things you <u>must</u> change and <u>should</u> change on page 13, or list three things you <u>need</u> to change now:

1.

2.

3.

In column one below, chose which of the following ways the consequence of **not** changing would likely affect you. Then in column two, chose how much it would impact you by choosing a level from 1-7 based on the chart below. Repeat this exercise for each change listed.

Consequence
(*Check all that apply*)

Impact
(*Choose level 1-7 for each*)

___ Emotionally (feelings, mood)   _____

___ Psychologically (thoughts, outlook)   _____

___ Physically (health, appearance)   _____

___ Socially (friends, entertainment)   _____

___ Spiritually (faith, religion)   _____

___ Financially (possessions, career)   _____

___ Ethically (morals, character)   _____

Impact Levels:

1. Almost No Impact	2. Low Impact	3. Some Impact	4. Moderate Impact	5. Elevated Impact	6. High Impact	7. Extensive Impact

Examine the impact level of each consequence you indicated. The more consequences you chose and the higher the impact level of each one indicates that this change is not only related to something you value most, but it also has the "why" potential to motivate you to action. This "why "should be enough to sustain that action as well.

Based on the consequences and impact, clearly state the most powerful reasons, or why's, for making this change in your life or achieving this goal (i.e. "I may lose my spouse, job or life."):

_____

_____

_____

5. DISTRACTIONS

Whenever you start a new behavior and then fall back into your old habits, you may behave worse than when you started to change. In other words, you don't always go back to the same level; you go lower than previously. If you began with low self-esteem, for instance, a new disappointment or failure will only serve to reinforce it. One way to ensure the best possible consistency is to effectively eliminate distractions.

Distractions hamper our ability to focus, and they come in many forms, including:

1. **People** (actual and virtual): *meetings, phone calls, email, social media, text/instant messaging*

2. **Events** (see, hear or experience): *parties, entertainment, games, gossip, broadcast news, sleep, dining, trips, sex*

3. **Thoughts** (past, present and future): *daydreaming, false beliefs, fears*

Which of the above most affects you?

_____

Fasting

Try to go on regular fasts or breaks from people and event-related distractions for at least one week or more at a time. Here are some ideas for such fasts:

Media fast – no television, radio, Internet

Communication fast – no phone, e-mail, or messaging of any kind

Entertainment fast – no parties, games, trips, extra rest

Social fast – no social events, social media, discussion groups, meetings

As for thought-related distractions, here are some possible fasts:

"No" fast – rather than saying "no," say "yes" to an alternative idea or plan that you have in mind; rather than saying "no," tell people what you would prefer to happen instead; rather than saying "no" to children, tell them what they can do or what you would prefer them to do instead

"Yes" fast – rather than saying "yes" to the people you feel most obligated to satisfying, give them boundaries or limits to your assistance; rather than saying "yes," tell people what you would prefer instead; rather than saying "yes" to children, tell them how their request impacts you and to come up with an alternate request with your feelings in mind

"Fear" fast – each day, ask someone for something who will likely refuse your request; ask a stranger for what you need or lack that he/she may be able to provide; tell someone you've never told how his/her actions caused you to feel

Create My Own Fast

You can also create your own fasts based on your needs and shortcomings. What type(s) of fast do you need most?

_____

_____

_____

_____

_____

_____

What is your goal for this fast? (i.e. to gain more time to read or study)

_____

_____

_____

_____

_____

_____

What are some restrictions you plan to put in place (i.e. one TV show per night)

_____

_____

_____

_____

_____

Habits

A habit fulfills or satisfies an intense desire. A habit is derived from a stimulus that always causes the same response; it is a motivational pattern. For example, stress, a stimulus, can trigger a habit like smoking. Here is the model for a habitat:

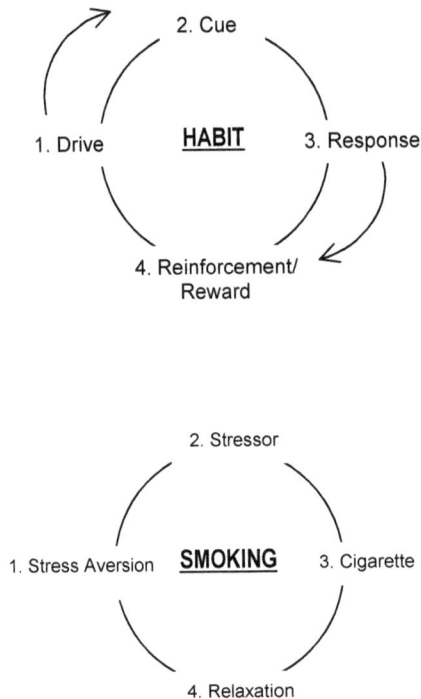

```
                    2. Cue

1. Drive          HABIT          3. Response

              4. Reinforcement/
                  Reward
```

```
                  2. Stressor

1. Stress Aversion  SMOKING   3. Cigarette

                  4. Relaxation
```

In step 1 in the smoking example, a person naturally seeks to avoid or relieve stress. When a stressor, or problem, occurs in step 2, the person decides to smoke in step 3. Because the cigarette reduced the person's anxiety in step 4, it reinforced or strengthened the person's desire to avoid stress. Once a habit is formed, an actual cue no longer has to trigger a response.

Habits, such as smoking, make change seem even more impossible because we typically get some type of satisfaction from them, whether emotional, physical, psychological, etc. In conditioning new behavior, we can focus on steps 3 and 4. In other words, we can try a new reaction (step 3), which may trigger an alternate type of reinforcement (step 4). For instance, instead of eating junk food when you're hungry, you eat fruit, which in turn, bolsters your health.

We can also focus on avoiding the prompt or cue (step 2) itself, so no reaction or reward will occur. Some people, for instance, try to stay busy to avoid certain people or situations that will adversely affect them. People also attempt this avoidance behavior when they ignore or deny something that is negative or potentially harmful.

What habit (i.e. overeating, overreacting, talking, lying) do you have that has interfered with or threatened your success and happiness?

_____

_____

Which of the following two ways is the best means to change this habit(s)? **Explain how**.

  1. Avoiding the stimulus, or trigger of the behavior

Example: Binge eating consists of brief episodes of uncontrollable eating. One cause of binge eating is going without food for long periods. Thus, a way to avoid binging is to eat small meals throughout the day.

_____

_____

_____

_____

_____

  2. Trying a new reaction

Example: Instead of binging on high-calorie foods, you drink a sizeable, healthy shake.

_____

_____

_____

_____

_____

6. MOTIVATION AS FUEL

Our **motivation** is based on *what we value* and *how much we value it*. We all have three main motivations. Remember, motivation is whatever someone hopes to accomplish, so it compels us to act. It's not motivation until a person acts or responds!

What motivates people is what they value most, and our main motivations are to:
- Live
- Love
- Lie

Because of this, certain types of "threats" work effectively to motivate us, including:
- Threat of death or injury
- Threat of the loss of love
- Threat of the truth being exposed

Threats (i.e. ultimatums, blackmail, etc.) operate on our *fear*. This is why fear is such an effective deterrent to accomplishments of any kind, and *faith* is such an effective remedy. Similarly, lack of forgiveness, or unforgiveness, is a major impediment to motivation. Forgiving yourself and/or others releases you from a lie, to love and back to life.

Have you ever wondered why a person seems to have no motivation? He or she seems to have no goals, enthusiasm, consistency or commitment. The reason could be any of the following:

- Internally motivated* person who feels great personal dissatisfaction or has false beliefs
- Externally motivated** person who is not getting what he wants or thinks he needs or deserves
- Person's "why" isn't big enough

*When someone does something for a physical reward, this is **extrinsic motivation**.
When someone does something for personal satisfaction, this is **intrinsic motivation.

Those lacking productivity may need to change their motivation, and here are four ways:

Conditioning	Positive/Negative Reinforcement, Punishment
Competition	Rewards
Coaching	Encouragement, Praise, Affirmation
Christ	Prayer, Faith

Conditioning means forming a new habit based on the negative or positive consequences of our choices. For instance, we are inclined to continue doing something if we like the outcome. I turn down a street because every time I do I see an attractive man or woman outside. We also stop or curb our behavior to prevent negative outcomes. I turn down Elm Street because every time I go down Lee Street, I'm late. Both competition and coaching can be forms of conditioning new behavior based on what people value or need, which motivates them. Christ can recondition our behavior through prayer by faith.

Which one of the following do you need for motivation? Rank them from 1 to 10 with 1 being the most important.

_____ Appreciation

_____ Acknowledgement

_____ Acceptance

_____ Negative Consequence

_____ Recognition

_____ Award/Prize

_____ Praise

_____ Encouragement

_____ Affirmation

_____ Faith

How can you cause or get the top three things (1, 2, 3) you identified above as necessary or important motivational factors? For instance, you can spend more time with positive or inspirational people.

If you can't get any of the above things from another individual, you must be willing to provide them for yourself. In other words, sometimes you may have to reward, encourage or believe in yourself.

Resources for Change

In order to reach your goal, you must recognize your resources. Some are limited while others are limitless in nature. When you treat the limited like the limitless, you'll abuse it. When you treat the limitless like the limited, you'll misuse it. "Denial" is the only thing that can inhibit the benefits and power of the limitless.

Limited
Opportunity
Vitality
Life/Time
Money

"Limited" resources must be used *efficiently*, meaning how does it work (quantitative)
"Limitless" resources must be used *effectively*, meaning does it work at all (qualitative)

Limitless
Awareness
Feelings
Thoughts/Ideas
God

Your level of *efficiency* will impact how you reach a goal (amount of time, organization, setbacks, etc.), not whether you reach your goal.

Efficiency is related to the method you have in place to reach your goals.
Are you organized?
Are you using your time wisely?

Your *effectiveness* focuses on if you reach your goal using resources (education, experience, etc.), not how you did it.

Effectiveness determines whether the method meets your goals.
Did you make the amount you planned?
Did you meet deadline?

Keep in mind that something can be efficient but ineffective. For instance, you can schedule a conference call rather than a physical meeting, but if you set it at an inconvenient time, no one may participate. It is also true that something can be inefficient but effective. Some vehicles, such as trucks, are very reliable but they are not fuel-efficient.

While efficiency and effective are different, they are both necessary in order to accomplish a goal in the best possible form. If you effectively meet your goal, but doing so cost lots of time or money, you should work on your efficiency. If you don't meet your goal, be prepared to change your method so that you can be effective.

Each day, set one "doable" goal. If accomplished, it builds self-confidence, which is a limitless resource. You'll need confidence for the bigger tasks.

What do you need to work on to reach your goals appropriately: efficiency or effectiveness? From the chart below, highlight or circle issues you need to overcome to reach your particular goal. You can even add your own items in the empty spaces provided.

Efficiency	Effectiveness
Time Management	Expertise
Money Management	Education
Information	Comprehension
Organization	Experience
Courtesy	Empathy
Fluency	Morals
Hope	Faith
Effort	Commitment
Rules	Attitude

On the next three pages, you will assess your time, money and thought management. In doing so, you should be better able to observe how you're using these resources. Furthermore, in aligning your entries with your values, you should be able to determine if you are living according to the things that you truly value most or you are distracted and so forth.

Once you're done with the exercises, you should have a better idea of your efficiency and how to use these resources, such as your thoughts or ideas, to become more effective.

Time Management

Log how you spend your time for at least two days, including work, outside activities, classes, sleeping, etc. Then try to estimate how much time was spent on the values listed on page 18.

6:01 am – 7:00 am   _____

7:01am – 8:00 am   _____

8:01 am – 9:00 am   _____

9:01 am – 10:00 am   _____

10:01 am – 11:00 am _____

12:00 am – 1:00 pm   _____

1:01 pm– 2:00 pm   _____

2:01 pm – 3:00 pm   _____

3:01 pm – 4:00 pm   _____

4:01 pm – 5:00 pm   _____

5:01 pm – 6:00 pm   _____

6:01 pm – 7:00 pm   _____

7:01 pm – 8:00 pm   _____

8:01 pm – 9:00 pm   _____

9:01 pm – 10:00 pm   _____

10:01 pm – 11:00 pm _____

11:01 pm – 12:00 am _____

12:01 am – 1:00 am   _____

1:01 am – 2:00 am   _____

2:01 am – 3:00 am   _____

3:01 am – 4:00 am   _____

4:01 am – 5:00 am   _____

5:01 am – 6:00 am   _____

Money Management

Log your spending for at least two days. Then align all your spending with a specific value listed on page 18.

Example
Amount: _$850_ Description: _Tuition payment_   Value: _Education_

Amount	Description	Value
_____	_____	_____
_____	_____	_____
_____	_____	_____
_____	_____	_____
_____	_____	_____
_____	_____	_____
_____	_____	_____
_____	_____	_____
_____	_____	_____
_____	_____	_____
_____	_____	_____
_____	_____	_____
_____	_____	_____
_____	_____	_____
_____	_____	_____
_____	_____	_____
_____	_____	_____
_____	_____	_____
_____	_____	_____
_____	_____	_____
_____	_____	_____
_____	_____	_____

Thought Management

Throughout your day, log what you are thinking in 15 or 30-minute intervals. Don't try to discover "why" you are thinking this or judge whether your thoughts or good or bad. The goal is to simply write the thoughts in a general, not specific, way. Then align all your thoughts with a specific value listed on page 18.

Example
Time: _10_   Thought: **_"What will we have for dinner?"_**   Value: **_Food_**

Time	Thought	Value
_____	_____	_____
_____	_____	_____
_____	_____	_____
_____	_____	_____
_____	_____	_____
_____	_____	_____
_____	_____	_____
_____	_____	_____
_____	_____	_____
_____	_____	_____

7. NEW DIATS

Establishing a goal requires us to make a change of some kind. Change can force us to:

- Alter the way we live to some degree
- Identify what we truly love
- Eradicate a lie and face the truth

In order to overcome and achieve your goal(s), you must sacrifice something. The sacrifice should be in the form of a DIAT. You'll have to have a strong enough desire and then exert your energy to focus on *only* what's important.

Don't criticize something you
- can't do anything about
- are unwilling to do something about
- haven't done before

Ignore things that are unimportant and also unessential to achieving your goal
- Schedule regular, set times for mandatory and essential activities
- Do nothing else during these times (no multi-tasking or interruptions)
- Do one thing – even something "small" – every day toward your goal
- Start over mentally every day if necessary, forgiving past failures while still learning from them (L.I.E. Process)

Ask for help
- Ask questions of people who have done what you're trying to do
- Assume nothing and keep asking until you understand
- Attitude is everything, so be humble, and you'll get the best from people. (Remember, other people don't have to help, so act like it)
- Admit you don't know all the answers and may need a mentor or motivator

Try to change only those things that are fully in your control, such as your
- Reactions to others
- Actions
  (Remember, acts of God and the will of others are out of your control)
- Attitude toward others or about a situation

See yourself as overcoming or achieving using
- Faith
- Visualization
- Self-Confidence

Design Your Own DIATS

Now it's your turn to state specifically what you plan to do on your new DIATS.

Don't criticize what or who:

_____

_____

_____

_____

Ignore:

_____

_____

_____

_____

Ask for help from:

_____

_____

_____

_____

Try to change only things in my control, such as:

_____

_____

_____

_____

See myself as overcoming using:

_____

_____

8. RELIGIOUS GROUP ACTIVITIES

Many times, people learn new concepts better within groups where they can share ideas and get encouragement. Within religious groups, it is always best to start with devotion, guided by a facilitator or leader. Devotion, or a devotional, prepares the mind and heart for a lesson.

DEVOTION

GOD IS...

Overview: Each individual will complete the sentence "God is…" with no more than two words to describe God's character. The goal is to devise a personal devotional title or moniker befitting one of the Lord's most praiseworthy roles in the participant's life.

Supplies: About 20 index cards and a fine point marker

Activity: The facilitator should tell the group to think about David who, at different times, called God his "Shepard," "Shield," "Rock" or "Defender" when having devotion. Abraham called the Lord his "Provider," Moses called God his "Banner," Gideon called God his "Peace," and Isaiah called the Lord his "Song." Likewise, the group facilitator should direct each participant to devise his or her own unique characterization of God.

As each participant arrives, the facilitator should ask everyone to think about a personal situation that he or she knew only God could have orchestrated. Then ask them to find one word to describe His nature or action in that situation. The facilitator should have ready on index cards the terms David and other righteous people in the Bible used to describe God. Read some of the names as a means to encourage each person's reflection. Immediately afterward, the facilitator should motivate the group's personal analysis with questions like:

- Do you remember a time when you had supernatural peace while going through a natural crises?
- Has there ever been a time when you or someone you love were healed from a condition that had been diagnosed as fatal, life threatening, incurable, or chronic?
- Did you ever wonder how you were able to love someone who for others would be unlovable?
- Have you always gotten what you deserved?

Finally, everyone should be directed to conclude the sentence "God is…" with **no more than two words** to describe God's character in relation to his or her own life. Keep in mind, articles (a, an, the) count as one word.

Examples:

God is <u>my source</u>.

God is <u>a friend</u>.

God is <u>the answer</u>.

After each person completes the sentence, group members can then talk about the particular instance that caused them to select the characterization.

<u>**Tips**</u>:

(1) Participants can use words from the index cards, but they should be encouraged to find their own unique characterizations. More than often, the word will be a noun such as friend or unifier. The group facilitator can add more index cards with example names of devotion used throughout the Bible to help individual reflection.

(2) As the group formulates their ideas, you may want to provide context for the origin of some of the terms used to reference God throughout the Bible. The facilitator can explain that Moses asked God for His actual name, and God said, "I Am" (Exodus 3:14). This is a complete sentence in the grammatical sense and a complete characterization in the spiritual sense. He is everything, but Abraham (Gen. 22:14), Moses (Exodus 17:15), Gideon (Judges 6:24) and others wanted to establish a personal moniker after their own experience with the Lord.

(3) The goal in this activity is to find *your own* devotional moniker for God. Thus, using personal pronouns such as "my" to help complement the sentence can help participants feel a greater devotion to the descriptive terms they choose.

(4) This exercise could be used regularly, asking participants to reflect over the past week, month, etc. In other words, participants can draw from new experiences and thus create new terms during each group session. Alternatively, individuals may seek to re-emphasize a name they had chosen previously but share a new experience surrounding the use of the name. This activity can be done alone daily in prayer and meditation, or routinely in a group setting.

LESSON

JESUS AT THE HOME OF MARY AND MARTHA
(Luke 10:38-42)

Lesson Focus: Put God first in everything

Key Verses:

"Seek ye first the kingdom of God and His righteousness, and all other things will be added unto you" (Matthew 6:33).

"Set your mind on things above, not on things of the earth" (Colossians 3:2).

"We give thanks to You, O God, we give thanks! For your wondrous works declare that Your name is near" (Psalm 75:1).

Overview of the Lesson

Each activity requires basic materials and preparation. Execute the activities in succession, as outlined below, in order to achieve the best comprehension and impact.

Lesson Sequence	Time	Activity	Supplies
Discovering My Values	Up to 10	**I Want...** **What:** Find out what they value most in their lives. **Why:** To discover what things may be interfering with their devotion and relationship to God.	"What Do I Value Most?" exercise
	Up to 15	**God Wants...** **What:** Find out what they *should* value most in their lives. **Why:** To discover their awareness of God's expectations.	Paper and pencils
Role-playing Biblical Meaning	Up to 15	**My Explanation...** **What:** Study the passage and have one person create an explanation for Jesus if he said to reduce the time and/or money spent for what the person values other than God (from handout). **Why:** To assume the same preoccupied role of Martha	Bibles, paper, pencils
	Up to 15	**Jesus' Response...** **What:** Have the person's partner prepare a biblical response, paraphrasing Jesus' message to Martha. **Why:** To assume the corrective role of Jesus.	Bibles, paper, pencils
Making Adjustments	Up to 15	**Priorities Pledge** **What:** Use the key verses as a basis to create a pledge to put God first. For example, write: I will seek God before I... and I know He will set my life in order" OR "I will set my mind on..., and less on..." **Why:** To take responsibility for shortcomings in their priorities and attempt to reorder them.	Index cards and pencils. Copies of the "Fruit of the Spirit" list.

Objective:

Although we have basic physiological needs, we are otherwise motivated by something we feel will fulfill us, or something we value. We give our undivided attention in the form of time, money or thought to those things we value or desire most. This lesson attempts to find out what people value most in their lives, so they can discover what things may be interfering with their devotion and relationship to God. Putting God first requires devotion to His *will, ways,* and *worship.* Most of us are committed to our own interests, forgetting that we were created to glorify God. Whenever we have an opportunity to glorify God through obedience or praise, we must choose to do so above our own desires.

Insight:

God gives much, but He requires little. He simply asks that we remember to honor Him in all that we do. Continually honoring God means to put His interests first. How would our lives change if we sought God's interests above ours in every situation? The thought for most of us is scary! You might think, "Will I have to become a minister or missionary?"

The truth is that putting God first is simple. We make it complicated by forgetting that through fellowship with God comes direction, inspiration, and blessings. While on Earth, Jesus healed, fed, delivered, encouraged, instructed, commanded, rebuked, or blessed all those who fellowshipped with him. He promised that all these actions would continue through the Holy Spirit after his departure. Therefore, today, we must allow the Holy Spirit to direct us toward God's interests.

So, no, the answer is that you don't have to become a minister or missionary in order to honor God in all that you do. You must simply call upon and follow the urgings of the Spirit in all that you do.

Facilitator Preparation

You will need to complete the "What Do I Value Most" exercise and pledge cards in preparation for the lesson. At times, you may have to share your responses with the group in order to incite the discussion. Groups, moreover, usually find it refreshing to know that the moderator is a peer, not a model of perfection.

Make sure that everyone understands the instructions on the worksheet as a first step in executing this lesson. The role-playing activity is crucial to grasping and applying the point of this lesson. Thus, you may need to demonstrate it with a group member before asking everyone else to do it.

Handing out new materials is usually a great trigger to signal the end of one activity and the beginning of another. However, certain group members may ignore or misunderstand this cue, so be prepared to also announce the need to move into another activity.

NOTE: These activities can be repeated each week because only one value from the worksheet is explored during the role-playing exercise. As the participants begin to make changes in their priorities, they may request a new "What Do I Value Most" worksheet at the beginning of class. Students may want to track their achievements by comparing their first worksheet to the last one.

Before Group Session:

Make sure you and everyone will have the "What Do I Value Most?" exercise (page 18).
Make sure you and everyone will have the "Fruit of the Spirit" list (page 47).
Make sure you have adequate pencils, index cards and blank paper for the group.

Organize chairs in a circle in the beginning, but keep in mind that the group members will be paired off for the role-playing activity.

Discovering My Values

I Want…

Ask the group to think about these questions:

1) On what do you spend a lot of time?

2) On what do you spend a lot of money?

3) On what do you give a lot of thought or attention?

Afterward, have the group complete the "What Do I Value Most?" exercise. Tell the group to be honest because they will *not* have to share their answers. Explain to them that their responses will, in some form, be used in the role-playing activity that coincides with the lesson.

Tip: Participants are not required to share with the group their answers from the "What Do I Value Most" worksheet. In fact, ask participants not to share their responses as they fill out the handout because the next activity requires some spontaneity in reference to the responses.

God Wants…

Once everyone says the "What Do I Value Most" exercise is complete on page 18, the facilitator should ask the group to think about what God values most. Immediately hand out the blank sheets of paper, and ask everyone to jot their responses.

Specifically ask the group to write on what does God want them to:

1) Spend a lot of time

2) Spend a lot of money

3) Give a lot of thought or attention

Give the group enough time to consider their responses thoroughly. Use 5 to 10 minutes to allow the group to discuss their responses to what God wants. The facilitator might ask, "Who would like to share their answers to what God wants?" Allowing a volunteer to begin the discussion will usually compel others to share with less apprehension. Keep in mind, not everyone has to share during this activity, for the purpose is to enlighten without making those who have less Bible knowledge feel uncomfortable.

Transition to the next activity by handing out a new blank sheet of paper and asking everyone to open their Bibles to Luke 10:38-42. Participants should keep track of their papers because they will be used in the next activity.

Role-Playing Biblical Meaning

My Explanation...

Begin by using a few minutes to have the group read the passage silently to themselves. Afterward, you read the passage aloud. Begin the discussion by explaining that Martha felt preparing and serving food for Jesus and the disciples was a top priority. In fact, Martha asked Jesus to reprimand her sister, Mary, who was fellowshipping with Jesus instead of assisting her. Jesus, however, wanted Martha to understand that fellowshipping with him at that moment took priority over housework. The Savior was in her house, and instead of worshipping him, Martha thought she needed to feed him.

Like Martha, most us are distracted from a true relationship, fellowship and worship experience with God. We spend much of our time working, entertaining, or resting. "What's wrong with resting?" you might say. Well, Jesus rebuked the disciples for sleeping on the night when they could have prayed with him just before his crucifixion. The group should then take their Bibles and find Luke 22:45-46. The facilitator or a volunteer should read the passage aloud.

Now begin the role-playing activity to better understand Jesus' message to Martha and applying the principle of putting God first in our own lives. Each person will need to find a partner to complete this activity. One person will act as Martha, and the other will be Jesus. Gender-specific roles don't matter because each person will be switching roles, so the person who acted as Martha will be Jesus and vice versa.

> **Tip**: Participants should be allowed to choose their partner in this role-playing activity. Allowing people to choose their partner will make them feel more comfortable when sharing.

Have partners turn their chairs to face each other.

> **Tip:** If there is an uneven number of people in the group, the facilitator may have to become one person's partner for this activity.

Instruct the person acting as Martha to write an explanation to Jesus about the thing(s) that he or she identified as top priorities (scored 10 or higher the "What Do I Value Most"). Have the person acting as Jesus say:

"Why do you spend so much time with that thing?"

Allow Martha to compose her thoughts on paper before Jesus asks,

"Why do you spend so much money on that thing?"

Again, allow Martha to compose her thoughts on paper before Jesus asks,

"Why do you give so much thought to that thing?"

Allow Martha to compose her thoughts on paper for the last time.

Once Martha has finished, she will read each response to the person acting as Jesus.

Jesus' Response...

The person acting as Jesus should compose a biblical response to his/her partner that paraphrases Jesus' message to Martha. Verses 41-42 of the passage stated, *"Martha, Martha,"* the Lord answered, *"you are worried and troubled about many things, but one thing is needed...."* To paraphrase this to the person currently playing the role of Martha, the person playing Jesus could say, "[Insert name], I know you are worried about your finances and work overtime as much as possible, but you also must remember to spend time each day in fellowship with God."

The facilitator should say to the group, "Now that you heard Martha's explanation, prepare on paper a reprimand based on Jesus' response to Martha or even the disciples. You can look over both passages for guidance. Try not to use the exact words. Simply extract the principle or the overall message in order to correct Martha. You can create three different responses or use one for all Martha's explanations."

Once everyone is done, instruct the partners to switch roles. Now Jesus will be Martha, and Martha will play Jesus. Each pair should execute the activity as it had been previously done. Tell everyone to let you know when he or she is finished.

Ask the group briefly to discuss how they felt after Jesus confronted them. Again, avoid using a standard starting point or person; instead a volunteer should share first. If the facilitator had to participate because of an uneven number of group members, he or she should begin the discussion if no one else immediately volunteers.

Transition to the next activity by giving each person three blank index cards. Then ask everyone to open their Bibles first to Matthew 6:33. Allow the group a minute to read the verse silently to themselves. Afterward, you read the verse aloud. Tell them to place one blank index card as a place marker in that page, and then turn to Colossians 3:2. Again, allow the group a minute to read the verse silently to themselves before you read it aloud. Do the same for Psalm 75:1.

Making Adjustments

Priorities Pledge

Tell the group they will use the three verses as a basis for creating a pledge to put God first. They should use the verse in Matthew to compose the <u>first pledge</u> to put **God's will** first.

Slowly read this example:

"I will seek God's will before I spend any money, and I know He will set my affairs in order."

Tip: The fruit of the Spirit (Galatians 5:22) list is just a suggestive list to use in creating the second part of the Putting God First Pledge statement.

Next, have the group look at "Fruit of the Spirit" list. Tell the group they will use the verse in Colossians to compose a <u>second pledge</u> to put **God's ways** first.

Slowly read these examples:

"I will set my mind on loving my family the way that God has shown me,"

        or

"I will set my mind on having more patience with my children as God has had with me."

Finally, tell the group they will use the verse in Psalm 75:1 to compose a <u>third pledge</u> to put **God's worship** first.

Slowly read this example:

"I give thanks to you, O God, I give thanks right now! For your wondrous _____

declare that you are near."

Once everyone is finished writing their own personal pledges based on the three Bible verses, tell them to place the pledge cards in a prominent or strategic location so they can read it throughout the day. Some people in the group may want to frame or decorate their cards.

Everyone should hold hands and pray for the invoking of the Spirit to carry out God's will, ways, and worship. Before dismissal, remind the group that when it reconvenes, everyone should be prepared to discuss how they adjusted their life to put God first.

FRUIT OF THE SPIRIT

You can use this list from Galatians 5:22-23 to complete the pledge activity. The Holy Spirit directs us toward God's interests. Calling upon and following the urgings of the Spirit will produce the expression of God's ways, or the fruit of the Spirit.

The Fruit of the Spirit is:

Love

Joy

Peace

Longsuffering

Kindness

Goodness

Faithfulness

Gentleness

Self-Control

www.ingramcontent.com/pod-product-compliance
Lightning Source LLC
Chambersburg PA
CBHW081547040426
42448CB00015B/3254